THE THIN BOOK OF ™

36O FEEDBACK
A Manager's Guide

Michelle LeDuff Collins, Ph.D.

What you are going to read

WELCOME TO the second in the Thin Book Series, a guide to the 360 or multi-rater feedback process. If you are new to the 360 or multi-rater experience, this book will guide you through the process. If you are a veteran of the 360, this book is the perfect companion for the next time. The brand or type of 360 available to you doesn't matter; this guide identifies the important commonalities and key points and will help you maximize the benefits of the process.

The book is designed to be easy to read with useful, "just-in-time" information. For those who are actually participating in a 360, the book offers concrete suggestions about choosing raters and making the most of the information you receive. We hope that you will finish the book with several good ideas on how to use your 360 results.

In keeping with our philosophy of Thin Books, we have also included three optional sections in the back of the book that contain information that might be useful at some point, but not necessarily when you begin the 360 process. The sections contain information about the broader uses of 360s, how a 360 is designed and administered, along with a sample report. Sections A and B answer many of the questions that managers have asked us.

The reference section contains additional resources if you wish to read more about 360 Feedback research and practices. In the meantime, we hope you find this book useful and informative.

Let us know how it goes...

Sue Annis Hammond, Editor
Thin Book Series
suehammond@thinbook.com

Michelle LeDuff Collins, Author
michellecollins@thinbook.com

To James R. Powers, Ph.D.

AUTHOR:
Michelle LeDuff Collins, Ph.D.

THIN BOOK SERIES EDITOR:
Sue Annis Hammond

COPY EDITOR:
Dana J. Williams

DESIGNER:
Alisann Marshall

ISBN 0-966537327
1st edition
August 2000

Contents

Chapter 1

What Is a 360 Feedback Process?

360 FEEDBACK is a process in which a manager receives both quantitative and qualitative performance feedback. The name refers to the 360 degrees of a circle and to the fact that the individuals invited to provide feedback to the manager represent the full "circle" of people with whom the manager regularly works. In addition to rating oneself, the feedback circle can include direct reports, peers, internal or external customers, and the manager's boss.

Potential Sources for 360 Feedback

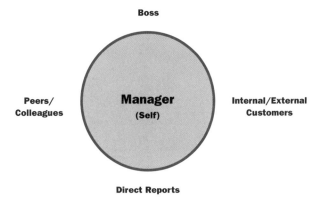

Boss

Peers/ Colleagues — **Manager** (Self) — Internal/External Customers

Direct Reports

6.

Although the process is usually known as 360 or 360-degree Feedback,[1] it goes by other names such as multi-rater, multi-perspective, or multi-source feedback. Internally developed tools can be called leadership, supervisor, peer, or upward-feedback surveys.

Commercially developed products have brand names like BENCHMARKS®, Campbell Leadership Index®, Competency Portfolio℠, Leader Behavior Analysis II™, Leadership Competencies for Managers ©, VOICES® Leadership/Impact™, and The PROFILOR®.[2] For the purposes of this book, we'll use the term 360 Feedback or, simply, 360.

Whatever the name, many of the processes and components in these feedback tools are the same, and we'll focus our attention on the commonalities.

How Does it Work?

The 360 process almost always includes a survey that lists items related to leadership and organizational success (for example, *Develops his/her people*), along with a corresponding scale to rate each item (for example, *Agree, Slightly Agree, Neutral, Slightly Disagree, Disagree*). Self-ratings and ratings from the participant's boss, direct reports, peers, and customers are typically compiled into a report. The results are combined and presented by rater category, which allows for insightful comparisons while ensuring that individual direct report, peer, and customer raters remain anonymous. Ratings by the participant's boss are also presented for comparison but are not anonymous.

7.

The 360 process may also include a goal-setting or development-planning component, which requires that the manager translate his/her results into a meaningful plan for future development. Some 360s are also linked to administrative processes such as performance appraisal, promotion, compensation, and succession planning (See Section A for more on this).

THE 36O TREND

In virtually all industries and in companies of all sizes, 360 Feedback has become increasingly popular. Some estimate that nearly every Fortune 500 firm is either using or thinking about using 360 Feedback.[3] This is the case because 360s fit the reality of the modern organization. Today, organizations are increasingly flatter, using more teams with multiple reporting lines. Employees are no longer satisfied with a single performance rating from a boss they may report to only on paper. As employees become more responsible for managing their own careers — *Brand You*, as Tom Peters describes it [4] — they are learning that to remain competitive, they must continually monitor their skills and choose what areas to develop further.

Some estimate that nearly every Fortune 500 firm is either using or thinking about using 360 Feedback.

8.

THE BENEFITS

360 Feedback offers many potential benefits to both the individual and the organization. Because the technique capitalizes on multiple perspectives, the results are considered highly credible and useful performance feedback.

For the individual, a 360 experience can help to confirm hunches about strengths and identify areas that need improvement. Being able to compare feedback from multiple sources helps participants contrast their self-perceptions with others' perceptions of them. But the benefits of this kind of reality check come with a challenge: As the *Fortune* article "360 Feedback Can Change Your Life" accurately points out, receiving the results can be surprising, powerful, and uncomfortable.[5] To help managers appreciate their strengths and not just concentrate on negative results, companies may provide feedback in one-on-one or group settings with trained coaches, facilitators, or psychologists. Such sessions can also help managers link 360 results to previous performance feedback, discover performance themes and issues, and understand how to use results to be more successful.

For the organization, a successful 360 implementation can improve communication among employees and help disseminate the organization's expectations with

> *Because the technique capitalizes on multiple perspectives, the results are considered highly credible and useful performance feedback.*

9.

regard to managers. The benefits can begin even before the 360 is implemented. A decision to implement the process signals that the organization desires and is committed on some level to improving its feedback mechanisms. Even the wording of the survey itself is instructive. 360 surveys typically group behaviors into broad success factors such as *Strategic Direction, Analytical Skills, Interpersonal Effectiveness, and Developing Others.* The very act of identifying these categories and then defining them by their associated behaviors — for example, *Considers future implications when making decisions* — gives the organization a common language with which to discuss performance.

IMPLEMENTING A DEVELOPMENT PLAN

Positive change is the ultimate goal of any 360. The true test of an individual's participation in the process is in taking action to achieve that positive change and to improve performance. To encourage and facilitate this change, most organizations require 360 participants to create and implement a Development Plan. The plan serves as the strategy for guiding the individual's improvement efforts and is a critical piece in using the results of the 360 to maximum benefit.

The Development Plan is used to record goals and desired activities for a designated period of time in the near future, usually a year. Since most managers learn on the job in challenging situations, it is important that the plan describe work situations in which the manager can showcase strengths and use and enhance skills that may need to be developed.

Once the Development Plan is written, it is the manager's responsibility to put it into effect. The company and the boss can provide various support mechanisms, such as an environment that promotes learning and the necessary resources, but the manager is accountable for taking action and carrying out the plan.

> *The manager is accountable for taking action and carrying out the plan.*

11.

Meet a 360 Participant

EXAMPLE ➤

In order to give the 360 Feedback process some
real-world application, we'll use the example of Stephen,
a hypothetical manager. What follows here is the background leading up to Stephen's first 360 experience. In
subsequent chapters, we'll explore Stephen's participation
in the actual 360 process in a more specific way as it
relates to the subject of each chapter.

Stephen began his career with a large diversified
financial-services company immediately after finishing
college. Initially, he worked in a branch location for two
years selling and servicing consumer loans. Then he
became branch manager and began managing others
while continuing to sell and service loans. Five years
later, when an opportunity at the regional level opened
up, Stephen was promoted. His responsibilities shifted
to managing multiple branches as well as managing
branch managers.

Stephen had been in his new position for about a
year when his company announced the 360 program.
Though he had never participated in one, Stephen had
been hearing about 360s for a few years before reading
in the company newsletter that all managers with
supervisory responsibilities would begin undergoing the
process. The company had acquired several smaller

companies and was launching multiple change initia-
tives to handle the integration, including using 360s for
development and company-wide management training.

Based on input from the company's senior management, a group of internal consultants designed the
360. An external consulting firm would be used to
administer and score the 360. Results were to remain
confidential but would be used for development planning
for the upcoming year. Each manager would attend a
one-day management development course based in part
on the key skills the company expected from its managers.

STEPHEN'S 360 AND
ADMINISTRATION PROCESS

Stephen's company launched a 50-item 360 survey
based on the company's expectations of all managers.
The process started with the company's top managers
and gradually cascaded through the organization.
Stephen was introduced to the survey when he rated his
boss. About three months later, it was his turn.
Instantly, those 50 items took on a whole new meaning.

The items were grouped into 10 categories,
called competencies, with five survey items per category.

13.

The survey incorporated both behaviorally worded and skills-based items with a corresponding five-point agreement scale (See Section B for more on scales).

Sample Items from Stephen's 360

LEADERSHIP SKILLS

Assigns projects that provide development opportunities.
NA   Strongly Disagree(1) Disagree(2) Neutral(3) Agree(4) Strongly Agree(5)

Provides clear direction.
NA   Strongly Disagree(1) Disagree(2) Neutral(3) Agree(4) Strongly Agree(5)

Delegates tasks to the appropriate people.
NA   Strongly Disagree(1) Disagree(2) Neutral(3) Agree(4) Strongly Agree(5)

Influences others by asserting his/her views.
NA   Strongly Disagree(1) Disagree(2) Neutral(3) Agree(4) Strongly Agree(5)

Is decisive when necessary.
NA   Strongly Disagree(1) Disagree(2) Neutral(3) Agree(4) Strongly Agree(5)

14.

Stephen received 20 survey packets on a Monday; completed surveys were due to the company's 360 vendor in two weeks. The surveys could be completed on the Internet, or could be faxed or mailed back to the vendor. Stephen began by completing his own self-ratings on the Internet. This gave him an opportunity to review the items before deciding whom to choose as raters. Although Stephen found it very easy to use the electronic version of the survey, he found it difficult to answer some of the items. He had never thought of his work behavior in the way the survey described things. Nonetheless, he completed the 50-item survey in 20 minutes and submitted it.

In the following chapters, we'll see how Stephen was rated and what he did with the results.

KEY POINTS

● *360 Feedback is a process in which a manager rates himself or herself and receives feedback from a variety of people with whom he or she works.*

● *The people who provide feedback are called raters and can include direct reports, peers, internal or external customers, and the participant's boss.*

● *Most 360 processes provide survey-based feedback, allowing results to be tabulated and presented by rater category for comparative purposes.*

● *360s have become increasingly popular because they fit many of the realities of today's organization.*

● *There are benefits both to individual 360 participants and the organization when 360s are successfully implemented.*

● *For a manager to get the most from a 360 Feedback experience, he/she must create and implement a Development Plan.*

Chapter 2

Choosing Raters

THE RATING process is rarely simple or straight-forward for either the manager or his/her raters. For the manager, figuring out whom to choose as raters and what criteria to use to pick them can be difficult. The mere act of soliciting performance feedback from others can be intimidating for the manager who might feel that he or she is suddenly in the spotlight or in a popularity contest.

Managers often overlook that raters also may find the process uncomfortable.

What managers often overlook is that on the other side of the experience, raters also may find the process uncomfortable. Evaluating the performance of others can feel awkward — just how awkward depends on the company's culture, the relationship between the rater and the manager, and how the results will be used. Additionally, raters often experience anxiety for any number of reasons: not wanting to hurt feelings, wondering whether the assurance of anonymity can be trusted, or worrying that they are perhaps not truly in the best position to adequately rate another's performance.

17.

CHOOSING 360 FEEDBACK RATERS

Most companies allow managers to choose their raters. If you have large peer and direct report groups and a limited number of surveys to distribute, who to choose (or eliminate) can be a tough call. The natural inclination, of course, is to select people you like (and who you think like you). This is where the process can begin to seem like a popularity contest and the point at which conscious or unconscious game-playing can ensue. People are inclined to choose work friends because they want to be perceived positively and to receive favorable 360 ratings; they think that having friends rate them will help accomplish this. They tend to forget, though, that "friends" can be brutally honest, especially when assured anonymity. Friends have intimate knowledge of your behavior across a variety of work situations and have fairly accurate perceptions of your strengths and weaknesses. So while it's fine to include work friends, remember that there are additional criteria to consider.

18.

Issues to Consider

■ Before you finalize your list of raters, complete the 360 self-rating. Doing this not only helps you familiarize yourself with the survey items, it helps you choose raters who might provide the best input.

■ Choose current co-workers rather than previous ones. Current work situations are likely to be different, and it may be difficult to draw clear conclusions from the results if data from previous co-workers are included.

■ Choose co-workers with whom you most closely work. The people who have had the most opportunities to observe your work behavior are in a better position to provide quality feedback.

■ Seeking feedback from colleagues and direct reports is a relationship-building outcome in itself because the mere act of asking for feedback from a peer perceived as a competitor may help change or enhance the relationship.

■ It is important that you believe your raters to be credible. You should trust that your raters will provide fair and accurate judgments,[6] otherwise it will be too easy to discount unfavorable results.

19.

Overlooked peers usually understand this better than do direct reports, who may feel that their opinions are not valued or that they were excluded on purpose.

If the number of surveys is limited, managers with large direct report and peer groups will obviously have to exclude a number of potential raters. Overlooked peers usually understand this better than do direct reports, who may feel that their opinions are not valued or that they were excluded on purpose. To overcome these negative feelings, some companies provide extra surveys so that all direct reports can participate.

Or you could devise your own strategy to solve this problem. You might follow the lead of some managers who, in their regular team meetings, randomly pick names of direct reports who will provide feedback. This approach makes the process public, and direct reports know how they were or were not selected. However you select your raters, if you cannot include all of your direct reports, clearly explain to everyone the rationale or method by which you make your choice.

COMMUNICATING WITH RATERS

Once you have selected raters, communicate your request in person, by telephone, by e-mail, or in writing. While this step may not be necessary in situations where people are aware that a 360 survey is coming, it does help prepare people in companies where 360s are not commonly used. A manager whose 360 is part of the preparation for an off-site leadership development course might send an e-mail message to selected raters letting them know to expect the survey. The message should succinctly explain as much as possible about the rating process: information about the 360 and how it will be used, when they can expect the survey, the deadline, the importance of honest input, the assurance of anonymity, and whom to contact if they have questions.

One of the most powerful and revealing aspects of 360 Feedback is the comparison of self-ratings to others' ratings.

SELF-RATINGS ARE IMPORTANT

One of the most powerful and revealing aspects of 360 Feedback is the comparison of self-ratings to others' ratings. The comparison helps you discover gaps between your self-perceptions and how others see you. Understanding the gaps is enlightening because it is difficult to be completely objective in your self-assessment. Indeed, the opportunity to know how others see you helps broaden your self-perceptions. [7]

21.

DIRECT REPORT RATINGS

The ratings by direct reports are another important part of the 360 process. In many cases, direct reports spend the most time with you relative to your other raters, and are certainly the most credible raters of your leadership skills. Even so, while some of you will welcome input from your employees, the role reversal may be a little unnerving for everybody, especially in traditional bureaucratic environments. Research shows that while direct reports are in the best position to assess leadership, communication, and interpersonal skills,[8] their ratings can be distorted, either positively or negatively, by the nature of the relationship and/or the power dynamic of the situation. For example, even when promised anonymity and assured that the ratings will be used for development purposes only, some direct reports fear retribution and slightly elevate their ratings.

If you sense uneasiness, do whatever you can to help your direct reports feel comfortable about the process by assuring them that you value and want their anonymous input.

22.

Peer Ratings

Research and experience suggest that understanding peer ratings is slightly less straightforward than other rating sources. The motivations of peers or team members can range from competitive to supportive to brutally honest, depending on the climate of the group and how the 360 is being used. In spite of these complications, research shows that peers observe more examples of work behavior across a variety of situations and that their ratings are a better predictor of who will be promoted than any other rating source.[9] Peers are likely to be effective raters of communication skills, interpersonal skills, decision-making ability, technical skills, and motivation.[10]

When choosing peer raters, ask approximately five people with whom you work most closely. This can help reduce the crush of surveys at the peer level when everyone is going through the 360 in a short period of time.

Research shows that peers observe more examples of work behavior across a variety of situations and that their ratings are a better predictor of who will be promoted than any other rating source.

BOSS RATINGS

While direct report and peer raters are very good judges of how work gets accomplished, bosses are typically better raters of what gets accomplished.

While direct report and peer raters are very good judges of *how* work gets accomplished, bosses are typically better raters of *what* gets accomplished. Since 360s tend to be better assessments of the how (for example, interpersonal and communication skills) than the what (i.e., results) of work, bosses may have a different perspective when rating some of the soft-skill competencies.

Furthermore, because boss ratings are usually not anonymous, they suffer from two of the same biases of traditional performance appraisal ratings: *restriction of range* and *leniency*.[11] In other words, boss ratings are not as likely to utilize the entire range of the scale and tend to be slightly elevated when compared with other rating sources.

Even though your boss may not have as many opportunities to observe you as your peers or direct reports, how he or she perceives you is still very important to your future.

24.

CUSTOMER RATINGS

Internal and/or external customers are also credible sources of information. Internal customers can provide useful feedback, especially if you work with them on an ongoing basis. External customers, however, don't always make the best 360 raters because they are usually concerned with a different or narrower set of outcomes than most 360s measure (for example, customer service, response times, and proactive problem solving).[12] External customers tend to have a difficult time making judgments about *how* work gets accomplished unless they have spent considerable time observing the manager's work. Sometimes external customers are reluctant to participate in 360s because they are not familiar enough with the organization's internal culture to know how the 360 will be used.

If you choose external customers as raters, you should have a separate rating category for them to check (usually *other*); this will allow you to consider their input separately.

25.

Stephen's Raters

EXAMPLE ▶

Like anyone facing a 360 and having to choose raters, Stephen had to make some decisions about what made the most sense for the process. His boss and ten direct reports were straightforward choices, and he immediately sent survey packets out to them. Counting his own survey, this left him with eight survey packets to distribute.

There were seven other regional managers in his peer group; however, there were other colleagues he worked with more frequently whose feedback he considered critical. One was a human resources person with whom he was partnering on an important recruiting initiative, another a technology person he worked with frequently, and another a regional manager from a different organization with whom he had worked closely during the past six months. Stephen decided to send rating packets to those three individuals, which left him with five surveys and seven viable peer raters.

To make the final decisions, he considered several factors: his relationship with each, how much he had worked with each, whom he respected the most, and who was the busiest at the time. Stephen knew that he did not need to use all the surveys and reasoned that he shouldn't in fact use them all because the other regional managers in his peer group were all going through the 360 process at the same time and were bound to be over-burdened.

Balancing all of these considerations, Stephen decided to send survey packets to the three regional managers with whom he had worked the most. One he knew very well, one he considered a rival, and the other he wanted to get to know better.

In the next chapter, we'll take a look at some of Stephen's ratings.

KEY POINTS

● *The 360 rating process is dynamic, affecting both the manager and his or her raters.*

● *Choose raters with whom you currently work and who can provide the most input on the survey items/categories.*

● *While you shouldn't necessarily avoid asking your work friends for input, you should go out of your way to include the opinions of others you respect.*

● *Each rating source has a unique perspective on your performance. Much of the value of the 360 process comes from exploring these multiple perspectives.*

Chapter 3

Understanding the Numbers

WE'LL USE some of the 360 results from our case example, Stephen, to help in interpreting your results. In this chapter, we'll look at the most common reporting techniques — *average scores* computed and presented in a variety of ways, and what you should look for when reviewing your own results. As you study the numbers, you will see that they only tell part of the story. The most informative part of any 360 process is in understanding the meaning behind the numbers. You can do this most effectively by having follow-up conversations with raters. Chapter 4 will help prepare you for those discussions.

SELF-OTHERS COMPARISONS

Comparing your self-ratings to those of your raters highlights alignment and discrepancies in perceptions. Significant differences signal areas that might require special attention.

The following graph shows Stephen's self vs. others (boss, direct reports, and peers combined) comparisons for two competencies. On the five-point scale, a half-point difference or more serves as a benchmark to distinguish meaningful differences. You will see that Stephen underestimates his *Administrative Skills* by almost two points (self = 2.4 vs. others = 4.2). The graph also shows that he overestimates his *Communication Skills* by more than one point (self = 4.8 vs. others = 3.4). These comparisons provide a useful pulse-taking exercise before diving into more specific results.

Stephen's Overall Average Competency Ratings

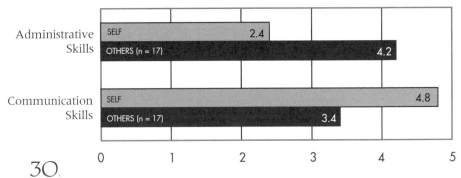

RATER CATEGORY COMPARISONS

Typically, the next type of analysis presents competency averages by rater category. Exploring agreement and lack of agreement among rater categories is very instructive. When you study your own results, here are some things to look for:

■ Are the results consistent by rater category?

■ Are there differences greater than one-half point between your self-ratings and any other rater categories?

■ Are there differences greater than one-half point among rater categories?

■ What do the ratings tell you about possible strengths (high ratings) and areas that might need improvement (low ratings)?

The graph to the right shows two examples of Stephen's average competency ratings. In the *Interpersonal Skills* competency, others rate Stephen about a 3 (boss = 3.4, direct reports = 3.1, peers = 2.9) while he rates himself a 4.6. Again, using the half-point or more as a benchmark, we see there is basically agreement among Stephen's raters on his interpersonal effectiveness. However, what's noticeable here is that Stephen seems to have a blind spot in this area and possibly an inaccurate sense of his impact on others. He responds to the discrepancy by noting it as a priority for further clarification.

In the *Leadership Skills* area, the ratings from Stephen's direct reports differ by a point from the other rating categories (direct reports = 3.2, compared with self = 4.2, boss = 4.2, peers = 4.2). Another red flag, this category presents Stephen with an opportunity to learn more about the meaning of the lower rating from his direct reports.

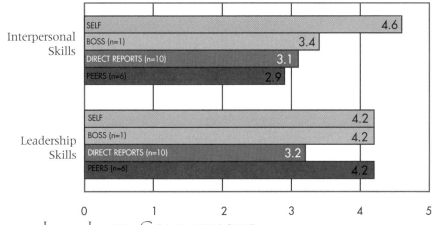

*Stephen's Competency Averages
by Each Rater Category*

ITEM LEVEL COMPARISONS

The next level of reporting is generally at the item level, where specific item averages are presented by rater category. This is the area where you will probably spend the most time trying to understand your results because it includes the most detail. To review item-level data efficiently, here are some things to look for:

■ What are your highest- and lowest-rated items?

■ What are your highest- and lowest-items by rater category?

■ What are the item-level ratings in your highest- and lowest-rated competencies?

■ Are the results consistent by rater category?

To get some practice learning what to look for, let's review a few of Stephen's highest and lowest items on the graph on the next page.

33.

Item Level Ratings By Each Rating Category

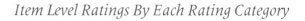

1. Establishes comprehensive plans

SELF	2
BOSS (n=1)	
DIRECT REPORTS (n=10)	
PEERS (n=6)	

7. Listens without interrupting

SELF	
BOSS (n=1)	
DIRECT REPORTS (n=10)	1.8
PEERS (n=6)	

10. Delivers effective presentations

SELF	
BOSS (n=1)	
DIRECT REPORTS (n=10)	
PEERS (n=6)	

20. Is decisive when necessary

SELF	
BOSS (n=1)	
DIRECT REPORTS (n=10)	
PEERS (n=6)	

0   1   2

Item 1, *Establishes comprehensive plans*, is one of his highest rated items by his peers (4.5) and the ratings by others are consistent (boss = 4, direct reports = 4.3). However, he rates himself much lower on this item (self = 2). Reviewing this item and the other items in the *Administrative Skills* competency helps him understand the large discrepancy between his self-rating and others' ratings in this area.

His peers rated item 10, *Delivers effective presentations*, lowest (2.7). His self, boss, and direct report ratings on this item are high (self = 5, boss = 4,

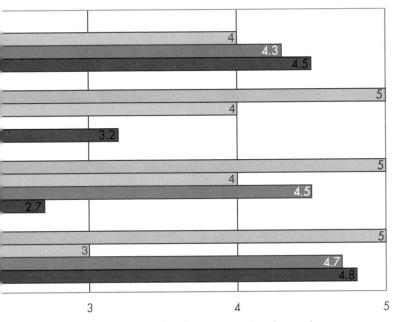

3   4   5

direct reports = 4.5). The discrepancy signals another candidate for further exploration, and Stephen puts it on his follow-up list.

One of his lowest direct report ratings was on item 7, *Listens without interrupting*. His direct reports rated this item 1.8 and the other ratings were not as low (self = 5, boss = 4, peers = 3.2). The lack of agreement suggests that he probably interrupts more or less depending on the person's status in the organization. He makes a mental note to pay closer attention to this issue.

35.

Stephen's direct reports rated item 20, *Is decisive when necessary*, highest (4.7). His peer rating and his self-rating were also high on this item (4.8 and 5 respectively). However, his boss rated him a 3, and Stephen took serious note and put this item on his list for discussion with his boss.

When you review your own results ask yourself, What is the feedback *in light* of the rating source? If you don't have your own report yet, use the results from 20 of Stephen's 50 items (Section C, page 88) to practice reviewing 360 results. Consider, for instance, the fact that Stephen's direct reports rated his delegation skills very low (page 89, item 18 = 1.8), while his boss, peers, and Stephen himself rated his delegation skills significantly higher (self = 4, boss = 5, peers = 3.8). Since his direct reports are probably in the best position to rate his skills in this area, Stephen concluded that he was not doing an adequate job of delegating.

SUPPLEMENTAL REPORTING METHODS

Norm Groups

Some 360 reports include the ratings of a norm group as a basis for comparison. The norm group may consist of all of the managers in the vendor's database, all of the managers at a certain level of management or from a certain industry in the vendor's database, or all of the 360 participants within your company. Frequently presented as percentiles or as average scores by item or by competency level, norm group comparisons can help you determine where you stand relative to other managers in general, in your industry, or in your company. Before considering what the comparisons mean, it is critical that you understand both who makes up the norm group and how the scores were derived.

Written Comments

Responses to open-ended questions can help you understand more about your numerical ratings and can show you what your raters consider important. The comments may not necessarily be designated by rater category, but they nonetheless offer a rich source of supplemental information. Look for comments that support and/or explain specific ratings; also look for comments about your overall managerial effectiveness.

Look for comments that support and/or explain specific ratings. Look for comments about your overall managerial effectiveness.

37.

LOOK BEYOND THE NUMBERS

Mostly High Ratings

In some instances, results can show mostly high ratings. Managers often have trouble making sense of this and may initially tend to think there isn't much room for improvement. If this should happen to you, look for *relative* high and low ratings. For example, when scores range from three to five, the threes may be possible development areas and the fives may be strengths. To test your hypotheses, have follow-up conversations with raters to clarify and confirm hunches.

Outliers and Low Ratings from One or More Rating Sources

Sometimes managers suspect that an "outlier" — usually someone who has rated them harshly across the board — has lowered their results. An outlier's ratings can obviously affect your average score, lowering (or increasing) your average; this is especially the case with small groups of three, as opposed to, say, ten raters. Keep in mind, a true outlier rates you the same way across the board. If *some* of your items are rated low, don't discount the feedback by attributing the ratings to an outlier.

38.

If you suspect an outlier, concentrate on looking for relative results. Since an outlier's impact is the same on every rating, the outlier has only slightly lowered (or raised) your average ratings. It's like adding or subtracting a constant since outliers typically go down the scale and rate all ones or twos (or fives). The actual numbers shouldn't matter as much as what behaviors, skills, or competencies stand out as relative strengths or development needs. So even if you suspect an outlier, your results should reveal the same relative themes.

Another issue with outliers is more psychological. If someone consistently rates you a one or two, you will wonder who they are and why they are seemingly out to berate you. Since raters are guaranteed anonymity, making an issue of it can affect both your credibility and the integrity of the 360 process. It is simply better not to worry about it and to move on to understanding what the results mean.

You may receive universally low ratings from one or more rating sources. Extremely low ratings from your boss warrant an immediate discussion. While this in fact rarely happens with boss ratings, it does happen with other rating sources. The challenge is to understand what is going on. Strained relationships are typically the cause; working on those relationships is an obvious response.

39.

KEY POINTS

● *Exploring self vs. others comparisons can help you see where your and your raters' perceptions are aligned.*

● *Looking for areas of agreement among rater categories reveals how aligned – or not – people are in their perceptions.*

● *List important discrepancies and either high or low ratings as a starting point for conversations with your raters.*

● *Written comments can help you make sense of your numerical ratings.*

● *The messages your results reveal about relative strengths and development areas are more important than the actual numbers in your report or whether you suspect an outlier.*

Chapter 4

The Meaning Behind the Numbers

NOW THAT you have some understanding of the layout of your 360 report and have an idea of how to interpret the results, think about how you are going to use those results to move forward. To benefit as much as possible from your 360 results, you should begin by considering a couple of important things: 1) how you are going to respond emotionally, and 2) what you need to discuss and clarify with your raters.

BE OPEN!

Most people are not accustomed to receiving so much feedback at one time. Because the experience can be overwhelming on several levels, it is best to prepare yourself. The best way to benefit from 360 results is to allow yourself to be somewhat vulnerable. Realize in advance that some scores will be flattering and others will come as unpleasant surprises. [13] If you are the type of person who eagerly anticipates feedback and is always open to suggestions, remaining open will be relatively easy. On the other hand, if you typically react defensively in feedback situations, you will have to consciously guard against this tendency. It is natural to feel defensive and to deny or rationalize unfavorable results. [14]

41.

Keep in mind, though, that to really derive benefit from the process and not just get through it, you need to be as open as possible. You might ultimately decide that the feedback is not accurate, but try to take it in and understand that this is how others see you.

First Step: Wait

Allow yourself about two weeks to absorb your results before sharing them with others. Some managers report actually taking their reports home and locking themselves in their studies in order to have the courage to look at their results. Don't be surprised if you react this way, too. Obviously, this is sensitive material, so start slowly.

Start by reviewing the report and then discussing it with your spouse/companion or your best friend. Every so often, share an item with someone who is close to you and see what he or she thinks. Oftentimes, they may hoot with laughter over the obviousness of the findings and give you an example that can help confirm it for you. Start with one of your higher-rated items and ask, "When

Allow yourself about two weeks to absorb your results before sharing them with others.

42.

did I do something like this?" Then slip in a lower-rated item and ask the same thing. By doing this, you will begin the process of 1) making sense of the data, and 2) getting confirmation that the results are accurate.

WHAT TO SHARE WITH OTHERS

Managers react differently to sharing their results. Some find it easy, others find it difficult. Some managers make copies of the entire report and hand it out to all of their raters or make transparency copies and present the results at a team meeting. Some managers are much less forthcoming. In one instance, a senior vice-president was suspected of never having read his results. Since going through the 360 process about two years ago, he has never acknowledged to his peers or direct reports that he received the feedback. And because their feedback was not entirely positive, they do not have the nerve to ask. In another instance, a project team had rated their boss for four years during the annual 360 but had never heard a word from her about the process or her results.

Suffice it to say that ignoring critical feedback is a potentially dangerous response. To do so can stall a promotion or raise, or worse, lead to your dismissal.[15]

43.

SAY SOMETHING

Most managers feel comfortable discussing their results in general terms. Acknowledging that you have received your results is a bare minimum.

Fortunately, most managers are somewhere in the middle of the extremes, neither sharing all nor saying absolutely nothing. But even for these managers who have a balanced response, it's common to have difficulty knowing what to say and to whom. Most managers feel comfortable discussing their results in general terms. Acknowledging that you have received your results is a bare minimum. Managers often prepare a short, semi-rehearsed story about what the experience was like; what they learned about their strengths and development needs; and high-level things they might have learned from their peers, direct reports, etc. (See Stephen's section for an idea of how to "script" a response that acknowledges you have received the feedback and thanks your raters for participating.) Once you've shared your results, go a step further and ask for additional feedback.

ASKING FOR FURTHER FEEDBACK

Asking for additional input can help you see even more clearly how other people perceive you and what they see as important. The report is a great opportunity to begin to dialogue with others about what the results

44.

mean, especially if some of your results are ambiguous or conflicting. These conversations can also help you learn more about performance expectations without compromising the anonymity of your raters.

The purpose of these discussions is not to confront your raters about their individual ratings or to reveal your specific results but to enlist their help. For feedback on areas that may be particularly sensitive to you, such as low interpersonal skill ratings, ask someone you really trust and whom you know will be honest with you.[16]

Using your 360 results as a starting point, ask for *best practice* examples. Begin by asking a few questions in each item or competency area (fill in the underlined portion with the appropriate item).[17] Here are some examples:

- *Can you tell me about a time when you observed a manager who was really good at delegating to the appropriate people?*
- *How did they do it?*
- *What did they need or have in order to do it well?*
- *How did the direct reports respond?*
- *What kind of results did that manager get on a regular basis or as a result of this?*

45.

By looking for *best practice* examples, you are not asking people to reveal their specific ratings or to beat you up with examples of when you didn't do something. Rather, you are getting solid data from others about what *best practice* behavior looks like so that you have solid ideas of *what to do* instead of *what to stop doing*. These *best practice* conversations also help the other person — be it your boss or a direct report or a peer — to clarify and articulate what he or she thinks is a good example. Chances are, this will lead to further discussion of how this behavior fits in your current job, your next job, the organization's culture, and why it is so important. You also get feedback because you are asking for it in a way that most people are willing to answer.

If you put the feedback to use and people see visible changes, they are more likely to provide input in the future.

Another goal of the discussions is to model what it looks like to ask for and receive ongoing feedback. 360 Feedback is only a starting place, a catalyst, for changing how people in the organization communicate. Let your raters know what you are trying to improve. If you put the feedback to use and people see visible changes, they are more likely to provide input in the future.[18] If you'd like to learn more about asking for and receiving feedback, refer to one of the Center for Creative Leadership's guidebooks, *Ongoing Feedback: How to Get It, How to Use It.*[19]

46.

Stephen's 360 Results

Stephen was fairly comfortable with most of his results, but overall he had mixed reactions to the process. He knew it was a lot to take in at one time and he needed a break from thinking about it. But not thinking about it was easier said than done, and he began airing some of his concerns about his low interpersonal skill ratings with his wife. His wife was not at all surprised by the feedback and told him so: He really could be difficult to get along with. During their discussion, she gave him examples of situations in which he had unknowingly turned people off by not listening to them or by not being open to their opinions. She also provided many examples of how well his opinions and advice were regarded by their friends.

Stephen had given himself two weeks to think about the results. This proved enough time to absorb, reflect, and accept. During those two weeks, he tried to pay close attention to the impact he was having on others. He had fun giving his wife nightly reports on small things he did at the office, such as asking for and actually listening to other people's opinions, and he commented to her that it really seemed to be making a difference in how people were responding to him.

47.

He began to tune in to a talk show while he was driving to work to practice active listening. He listened to what the host and callers said and tried to put their opinions into his own words. He began to notice that when someone stated an opinion that he disagreed with, his first response was to discredit the person in his head. He learned instead to take a deep breath in order to keep on listening. By doing this, Stephen was in fact engaging in an informal low-risk, no-cost creative development exercise.

WHAT STEPHEN TOLD OTHERS

Soon after Stephen received his results, but before he was ready to begin working on his Development Plan, he decided to acknowledge to his raters that he had read and thought about their feedback. He found the idea of sharing his reactions to the process uncomfortable, so he jotted down a few things to say. He found it easier to broach the subject once he had a "script." Here's what Stephen practiced telling others:

48.

"I recently got back my 360 results. This was my first experience receiving so much feedback, and I was surprised at some of what I learned. It's interesting that in general, people seem to see me pretty similarly and in ways that I wasn't entirely aware of until now. For instance, everybody thinks I'm pretty good in the administrative area, and I don't really see myself that way. On the other hand, I overestimated how people see some of my communication skills. That was a real surprise, and I'm working on understanding more about my specific results. I also liked the write-in comments. They helped me know that there's a lot I'm doing well and should continue to do. Thanks for taking time to provide your input."

MOVING FORWARD

When Stephen was ready to move forward, he used one of his team meetings to generate ideas for his Development Plan. He told his team that he would be trying harder to provide them with direction, to match them with the kinds of assignments they needed, and to delegate more. He asked them to give examples of when he had done a good job of providing direction. What did it look like? How did it impact the team? Would they point out future opportunities for him to provide more direction? He also asked them for *best practice* examples. His team was impressed that he had taken time to get

49.

more of their input and to include them in generating solutions. His discussions also went well with his boss and his peers. He wanted clarification on some of his peer ratings, so he scheduled separate lunch meetings with two of his raters. He asked them both for *best practice* examples. The conversations helped him understand his results better, especially how it was that the peer group had rated him differently in some areas. In one case, his colleague revealed that she too would be trying to improve her skills at developing others and they brainstormed ideas about what they might do differently with limited resources and in a geographically dispersed branch system.

Stephen's discussion with his boss, Margaret, focused more on the future and where Stephen saw himself going in the company. While he was satisfied with his current position, Stephen did want to be considered for future promotions and wanted to know how he could best prepare. Margaret gave him several examples of ways he could use his strengths as well as work on areas that needed improvements.

50.

For example, part of why Stephen received such high ratings in the administrative area was that he was a master of administration. But he had trouble delegating. He had been promoted because of his effectiveness, but he wasn't using what he knew to get the work accomplished through others. He was beginning to understand how there was a flip-side to this strength. Even though he wasn't fully aware of it, it was also a weakness.[20] All of his discussions helped him see that this was the key reason he received low ratings from his direct reports in the *Leadership Skills* area. Margaret used herself as an example of a manager who was very effective at delegating work to her people and supporting them in accomplishing it. Stephen realized that if he tried delegating, he would free up some of his time to engage in more strategic types of work. He also knew that if he didn't improve his delegation skills, he had little chance of future promotion. This became his top development priority.

> *He was beginning to understand how there was a flip-side to this strength. Even though he wasn't fully aware of it, it was also a weakness.*

51.

KEY POINTS

● *Approach receiving your results with an open mind.*

● *Before drawing firm conclusions, allow yourself time to absorb results and to do some reality checking with others with whom you feel comfortable.*

● *Be prepared to discuss overall results with your raters and to acknowledge their input.*

● *Solicit input from others to clarify ambiguous results.*

● *Go a step further and use the conversations to identify best practice examples so that you get tangible ideas of what to do in the future.*

● *Show you are committed to the feedback process by using people's input and asking for ongoing feedback.*

Chapter 5

Translating Results Into Action

AFTER YOU'VE taken time to get a good understanding of your results and speculated about which of
the messages are most important, the next critical step
is to devise a strategy for using what you've learned.
Putting a Development Plan on paper is a critical part
of the process; committing to taking the time to actually
do it is the first step.[21]

Anecdotal evidence suggests that some managers
only go through the motions with the Development Plan
and don't give it the attention it deserves. It's possible
that many managers fall into this trap because there is so
much emphasis on the earlier — and easier — stages (who
to give surveys to, for instance). By the time they get to
the Development Plan, they have little energy for asking
for the input they need and for following through with a
draft of a meaningful plan. Fortunately, there are specific
easy-to-implement ideas to turn results into action once
you've had the kinds of discussions described in Chapter 4.

Most 360 Feedback processes include a written
Development Plan with sections on goal-setting, summarizing strengths and development areas, and listing
developmental activities that most effectively use
strengths and shore up weaknesses.

53.

In this chapter, we'll work through parts of Stephen's plan. In the end, not all of the things he learned from the process or ideas he generated from conversations with others were included in his formal Development Plan. But that didn't diminish the importance of all the information; Stephen had already put some of the suggestions into action; others he would try in the future. Only the most critical areas — the ones that were most important in achieving his goal in the upcoming year and that would require resource allocation — were included in his written plan.

GOALS

Your Development Plan should be based on one or two goals for the upcoming year. For the plan to work, you should have some end in mind, and you should have some ideas about your goals for the next year or two. Your goals may include such things as a promotion, lateral move, successfully completing the project you're managing on schedule and under budget, changing to a different type of work or role, changing to a different industry, having a more flexible work schedule, working less overtime, handling the demands of the job better, making more money, or staying put. There is probably something you would like to improve on to be more effective — whether it's getting more organized or being more of a team player. Even if you haven't consciously thought about it, your 360 results and conversations with others can help you generate ideas. Prioritize your ideas and choose one or two objectives for the coming year. You are more likely to succeed at your goals if you narrow your focus.

STEPHEN'S GOAL

Our hypothetical manager, Stephen, was very happy with his current position, but he had higher aspirations for the next three to five years. His goal for the following year was to start preparing himself for the next move by improving his skills at delegating and providing direction, which had received mixed reviews in his 360 results. He also realized that his strengths could become potential weaknesses if he didn't start to use them differently.

EXAMPLE

55.

BUILD ON YOUR STRENGTHS

Most Development Plans allocate space for summarizing key strengths and for describing ways to use them to be even more effective. Your key strengths are the things that you should continue doing, the things that will have the greatest impact on your success.

Ask yourself these questions:

- *What can I do more of to achieve my current goal?*
- *Which ideas/issues stood out in my follow-up discussions?*
- *What are my highest-rated items or competencies?*
- *How can I leverage my strengths to shore up my weaker areas?*

Refer back to the conversations you had with your raters to decide on what's important. Keep your list crisp; focus on up to three important areas so that you will be able to devote quality time to them in the upcoming year.

Look at Stephen's list to the right, and try to describe your key strengths similarly. Keep your descriptions at the behavior or skill level. Behaviors and skills are easier to target and change than more abstract descriptions of your strengths.

Your key strengths are the things that you should continue doing, the things that will have the greatest impact on your success.

56.

Stephen's Key Strengths

Administrative Skills

■ *Establishing comprehensive plans and being able to adjust plans to meet changing priorities.*

■ *Managing information and resources effectively.*

Leadership Skills

■ *Ability to influence by asserting opinions.*

FOCUS ON WHAT TO IMPROVE

Deciding on which areas to improve on should be based both on 360 results and your follow-up conversations with your raters. Before you prioritize, think about your current goal and ask yourself these questions:

■ *What improvements will advance me the most toward my goal?*

■ *Which ideas/issues stood out in my follow-up discussions?*

■ *Which best practice ideas can I implement?*

■ *What are my blind spots?*

■ *What are my lowest-rated items or competencies?*

Answer by listing behaviors or skills. Focus on up to three areas that would really make a difference if you were successful in improving them.

EXAMPLE

Let's turn to Stephen again to see what he chose to improve. In the short term, there were many areas in which he hoped to improve. After considering what was really important to him in light of his current objective of developing his leadership skills, Stephen arrived at the list below. He realized from his conversation with his boss that not strengthening these areas would stop future promotions.

Stephen's Development Areas

Leadership Skills
- *Provide clearer direction to my team.*
- *Delegate with development in mind.*

Interpersonal Skills
- *Listens without interrupting and be open to different points of view.*

58.

ACTION PLANS

Some companies worry about 360s because of this phase of the development planning process. What classes will managers request and what they will it cost? Their concerns are justified but illustrate the limited view we all have about development. Most of us think that development only takes place in a classroom and that everyone will select an expensive class that will involve even more expensive travel. But the best learning sometimes takes place on the job, in real-life work situations that stretch us beyond our comfort zone. You'll see that very quickly when you start generating your *best practice* ideas.

Your objective is to determine, along with your boss, which on-the-job activities or situations would allow you to exercise your strengths and work on building up your weaker areas. In some cases, formal training may be necessary, but think creatively and refer to your *best practice* ideas. You might also refer to some helpful books that offer excellent development suggestions: *The Successful Manager's Handbook* , [22] *The Successful Executive's Handbook,* [23] and *For Your Improvement*™. [24] These books are great resources for generating additional ideas for your Development Plan and include lists of books and articles, audio tapes, classes, and on-the-job activities.

> *The best learning sometimes takes place on the job, in real-life work situations that stretch us beyond our comfort zone.*

59.

Looking at examples from Stephen's plan (two strengths and two development areas) and how he used them, we notice that his plan showed he was committed to development because one of his action items was to continue to ask for feedback on an ongoing basis.

KEY STRENGTHS	ACTION PLANS
Administrative Skills *Establishing comprehensive plans and being able to adjust plans to meet changing priorities.*	■ Join headquarters team that creates and executes plans for new company acquisitions. ■ Help branch managers develop in this area by delegating planning activities.
Leadership Skills *Ability to influence by asserting opinions.*	■ Create and communicate a clear vision for my organization. ■ Involve my team in the shaping of the vision. Adapt the vision to the needs of the team.

KEY DEVELOPMENT AREAS	ACTION PLANS
Leadership Skills *Provide clearer direction to my team.*	■ Present regional goals and objectives to team and get their input on how to accomplish them. ■ Ask team at monthly meetings for ongoing feedback on providing direction.
Leadership Skills *Delegate with development in mind.*	■ Provide "stretch" assignments to direct reports. ■ Let them try it "their way." Be available to answer questions and provide coaching. ■ Have Emma Mills attend regional meetings in my absence.

RESOURCES

Action plans typically require the involvement of others as well as the use of resources. When you write out your plan, you will also want to outline who and what you will need to accomplish your action items. Ask yourself these questions:

■ *Who will I need to involve to do the things I'd like to accomplish?*

■ *What are the time frames needed to put my plan into action?*

■ *Are there target dates by which I'd like to have things accomplished?*

■ *Will I need time away from the office to take a course?*

■ *What will it cost to fund my development activities?*

The following page gives an example from Stephen's plan that shows what kinds of resources he would need in order to participate in the acquisition team meetings.

61.

ACTION PLAN	RESOURCES NEEDED
Join headquarters team that creates and executes plans for new company acquisitions.	■ Two days per quarter away from the office to spend at headquarters (time away from office, airfare, hotel, meals). ■ Develop Roberta Peters to take over my responsibilities in my absence. ■ Time as needed on an ongoing basis to participate in conference calls and acquisition planning projects (approximately one day per month).

HOW YOUR BOSS CAN HELP

Your boss can help you get the resources you need and help you generate ideas for action planning. If we go back to our hypothetical manager, Stephen, we can see the ways in which his boss, Margaret, facilitated his 360 goals. His boss knew that the acquisition team needed an additional member. While discussing his feedback results with him, Margaret realized that if Stephen was interested in the opportunity, it would be a great fit for both the team and for Stephen. He would gain exposure with managers at headquarters and grow professionally, and the team would really appreciate his talents.

Stephen and Margaret talked through the details of what he planned to do and the resources that would be required. They agreed that Stephen would take responsibility for his plan and for communicating his progress to Margaret. Stephen also committed to asking her for ongoing feedback in the future. They both felt that the 360 Feedback process had been a major time investment but that it had potentially great dividends.

FINAL THOUGHTS

The information and techniques in this book should make your 360 process a positive growth and development experience. In reviewing your results and consulting with others, you may lose sight of the fact that you have been doing many things very well. Take time to acknowledge your talents and to create a plan for development that capitalizes on your strengths as much as it shores up your development areas. As the *Fortune* article says, "360 Feedback Can Change Your Life."[25] Use the results to find creative ways to become even more successful.

KEY POINTS

● *Commit to creating a written Development Plan.*

● *Base your plan on a goal for the upcoming year.*

● *Your plan should include ways you can use your strengths and improve your weaker areas.*

● *Look for ways to learn from on-the-job situations and use best practice examples as a useful starting point.*

● *Increase your chances of implementing the plan by discussing it with your boss (or the appropriate person in the organization) to get the resources and organizational support you need.*

Section A

Common Uses of 360s

THIS SECTION outlines common uses of 360 Feedback. Depending on its strategic goals, a company might use 360 Feedback for any number of objectives. For simplicity's sake, we'll describe each rationale separately, but you may find the lines blurred in real-world applications.

MANAGEMENT DEVELOPMENT

The most popular application for 360 Feedback is for management development. Management development experiences focus on enhancing a person's leadership capabilities through a number of alternative strategies, including assessment and feedback. The following description of Company A provides an example of a typical management development 360 process.

Company A: Example of 360 Process Used for Management Development

Participants	All managers who have direct reports
Participation	Required
Tenure in Position	Minimum of three months
Frequency	Annual basis (company anniversary date)
360 Training	Group sessions for participants
Rater Selection	Participant chooses raters
Rater Anonymity	Assured to peers, direct reports, and customers
Results Processed	External vendor
Feedback Report	Delivered in one-on-one or group sessions (depends on management level)
Who Sees Results	Participant only
Personnel File	No copy retained in file
Development Plan	Required
Development Discussion	Recommended with direct reports and boss

When 360 Feedback is used for development, the
common practice is that no one in the company sees the
feedback report except the 360 participant and a neutral
party who processes and distributes the results (usually
an external vendor and/or human resource development
professional). However, the participant is typically
expected to share a written Development Plan, based
on the results, with his/her boss. Some companies go
a step further and recommend that participants discuss
their overall results — for instance, three strengths and
three development needs — with their boss and/or direct
reports so that there can be additional accountability and
communication.

PERFORMANCE APPRAISAL AND OTHER ADMINISTRATIVE PURPOSES

Some companies link 360 Feedback results to performance appraisal, compensation, succession planning, or promotions. They may opt to use 360 ratings as part or all of a formal performance appraisal. Because 360s represent a radical departure from traditional performance appraisals, many companies start slowly, using 360s for development only, then gradually building in accountability and a direct link to administrative decisions such as compensation and promotion.[26] Company B (right) provides an example of how a 360 process might be implemented to accompany a performance appraisal process.

Company B: Example of 360 Process Used as Part of Performance Appraisal Process

Participants	All managers who have direct reports
Participation	Required
Tenure in Position	Minimum of three months
Frequency	Annual basis
360 Training	Group meetings for participants and video for raters
Rater Selection	Participant chooses raters with boss's approval
Rater Anonymity	Assured to peers, direct reports, and customers
Results Processed	Internally
Feedback Report	Delivered in one-on-one or group sessions (depends on management level)
Who Sees Results	Participant and boss
Personnel File	Copy retained in file
Development Plan	Required
Development Discussion	Required with boss and recommended with direct reports

When 360 Feedback is used for performance appraisal, the common practice is that the participant uses the report for development planning, while the boss has the discretion to use it to complete performance appraisal ratings.

69.

OTHER USES OF 36O FEEDBACK
Culture Change Initiatives

A company whose current strategic goal is to change its culture may opt to implement a 360 process. A company might use the 360 early on as a diagnostic tool to gather baseline data for later comparison. Companies may also use the 360 to introduce actual culture changes, such as subtle shifts in desired leadership qualities (for example, *Developing others, Building customer relationships,* and *Collaborating with others*). Another frequent goal of initiating a 360 process is that people begin sharing constructive feedback about individual performance issues.

Assessment Centers

An Assessment Center is a management assessment and development experience used to evaluate a manager's job-related strengths and development needs. The process relies on multiple exercises and multiple assessors. For companies wishing to provide an enriched management assessment and development experience, 360 Feedback can be an important piece in the comprehensive process.

Assessment Centers are used for high-potential manager development, succession planning, promotion, and career development. They are administered over a few days by trained professionals. Typical Assessment Center exercises include an in-basket exercise, a role-play simulation, an in-depth interview, work-related psychological assessments, 360 Feedback, and team or group exercises. The results from all of the exercises are integrated, and the themes presented to the manager through a combination of one-on-one feedback and a written report. Results from the 360 often help connect the Assessment Center exercise results with patterns reported by co-workers.

Leadership Development Courses

A 360 can also be used as a component in internally or externally delivered leadership development courses. Ranging from a day to a week or more, these courses combine lectures and group and individual exercises to help managers become more effective leaders. Companies often use internally developed courses to bring everyone who reaches a certain level of management

71.

up to the same standard. 360s may also be used to see how well managers' leadership skills are aligned with the company's expectations. In externally developed programs — in which managers from a variety of industries focus on building general leadership skills — the 360 can provide a manager with comparative data on where he or she stands with regard to those general skills.

High-Potential Programs

High-potential manager programs often use 360 Feedback as part of a menu of options available to the participants to help determine development needs and/or suitability for future assignments. In companies that use the 360 only for their high-potentials, a manager's participation in the process can be the first sign that he/she has been "tapped" for the program. 360 Feedback can provide high-potentials with valuable insight about how others perceive them.[27]

Coaching Programs

360 Feedback can also play a role in coaching programs. Typically delivered by external or internal consultants, coaching programs can help a valued manager develop or enhance skills in specific areas such as *Thinking more strategically* and *Delegating more effectively*. One-on-one coaching, often called "executive coaching," is a more targeted alternative for skill enhancement than a training class or a general leadership development program. Coaching participants vary from high-potential managers to solid performers whose continued success is important to the organization to managers whose careers may be in jeopardy if changes aren't made quickly. Many coaches rely on 360 results as part of their diagnostic assessment to determine where to focus.

The 360 Survey

FOR MANAGERS who would like to know more about item writing, scale construction, and survey length, and how these issues impact the feedback process, this section outlines the basics of the design and administration of 360 surveys.

HOW SURVEY ITEM ARE WRITTEN

360 items are usually grouped into categories called competencies. Competencies are the knowledge, skills, and abilities required for success and are a useful way to communicate performance expectations.

The competencies can be derived from management and employee input and/or based on general models of leadership. The items included under each competency heading typically have been researched extensively and found to identify an important aspect of behavior related to that competency.

Sample Competencies
with Corresponding Example Items

Administrative Skills Competency

■ *Uses information effectively.*

■ *Manages multiple priorities.*

Communication Skills Competency

■ *Is easily understood.*

■ *Listens without interrupting.*

EXAMPLE

Most 360 survey items are written in multiple-choice format: Respondents choose one response for each item, such as *Agree, Somewhat Agree, Disagree*, etc. Survey designers follow several guiding principles when writing the items. Survey items should:

■ Be clearly and concisely written.

■ Describe only one behavior or skill (for example, *Person delegates vs. Person delegates and gives feedback appropriately*) and not describe personal characteristics.[28]

■ Assess what they are intended to measure (items are generally piloted extensively and statistically analyzed).[29]

75.

Sample Survey Items Worded as Behaviors, Skills, and Personal Characteristics

EXAMPLE ➤

BEHAVIORS

Items worded as behaviors are the most tangible and, therefore, are more useful to the person receiving feedback. Examples of behaviors:

■ *Is decisive when necessary.*

■ *Establishes comprehensive plans.*

■ *Provides praise for a job well done.*

SKILLS

Items worded as skills are less tangible and present a less clear-cut indication of what the person receiving feedback should do differently. Examples of skills:

■ *Influences others' opinions.*

■ *Promotes positive relationships.*

■ *Is good at recognizing others' contributions.*

PERSONAL CHARACTERISTICS

Items worded as personal characteristics are the most abstract, the most difficult to change, and should be avoided with 360s. Examples of personal characteristics:

■ *Is dependable.*

■ *Shows a strong work ethic.*

■ *Is honest.*

76.

Many 360s include additional items written as open-ended questions. Raters like these types of questions because this format gives them an opportunity to provide feedback in areas not captured on the multiple-choice survey items; they like being able to illustrate or emphasize points in their own words. 360 participants also like open-ended questions because the responses provide rich supplemental feedback and frequently clarify ambiguities or inconsistencies revealed in the ratings.

EXAMPLE

SAMPLE OPEN-ENDED QUESTIONS

■ *What should this person do more of?*

■ *What should this person do less of?*

■ *Provide examples of how this person promotes positive relationships.*

■ *Provide comments about this person's effectiveness as a manager.*

77.

Rating Scales

Rating scales are used to capture raters' perceptions about whether, or how well, the manager being rated demonstrates the surveyed behaviors and skills. Most scales associate numbers with anchors (for example, 1 to 5, where 1=*Strongly Disagree*, 5=*Strongly Agree*); these are used to compute a numerical score. Some scales use only verbal descriptors, such as *Strongly Disagree* and do not associate the verbal rating with a numerical value; these descriptors are, however, later converted into numerical values for reporting purposes.

Rating Scales

Strongly Disagree, Disagree, Neutral, Agree, Strongly Agree

Never, Almost Never, Sometimes, Usually, Always

Not at All, Not Often, Often , Very Often, Nearly Always

Needs Improvement, Development Area, Meets Expectations, A Strength, Exceptional

Four-Point Scale

Strongly Disagree, Disagree, Agree, Strongly Agree

Six-Point Scale

Strongly Disagree, Disagree, Somewhat Disagree, Somewhat Agree, Agree, Strongly Agree

Scales can differ in the number of points and the number of choices that are included. Generally, scales range from three to 15 points. Most 360 designers use a five-point scale, or they use four or six points so that there is no middle point. By eliminating a middle point, survey designers overcome the problem of the raters' propensity to overuse the safest choice on the scale, the middle or average rating.

It's often debated whether to include a *Not Applicable (NA)* or *Don't Know (DK)* rating choice. The rationale here is that raters need to be able to distinguish items that aren't relevant or that they haven't observed. The advantage to including *NA* or *DK* as a rating choice is that these choices are not computed in the item's average score. When there is no *NA* or *DK*, raters often choose the middle point of the scale to express *Not Applicable* or *Don't Know*; this can lead to confusion about what the middle point actually represents.

SURVEY LENGTH

The length of a 360 survey affects the rater's motivation to complete it, the time it actually takes the rater to complete it, and the rater's overall impressions of the process. Longer surveys, especially those with more than 100 items, can take up to an hour to complete. And the time it takes to complete 360 surveys can multiply very quickly for boss and peer raters, some of whom receive rating requests from more than ten individuals at one time. Because of this, many companies who use the 360 for all management employees opt for a shorter survey or exclude one rater category altogether, such as peers.

360 SURVEY ADMINISTRATION

The survey itself can be administered in a number of ways, including one or a combination of the following:

■ Paper and pencil (mail or fax responses)

■ Telephone

■ Disk-based

■ Intranet/Internet

Raters are typically given two weeks to complete the survey. Once the established cutoff is reached, a feedback report is generated.

81.

Section C
*S*tephen's Data

Stephen's Overall Average Competency Ratings

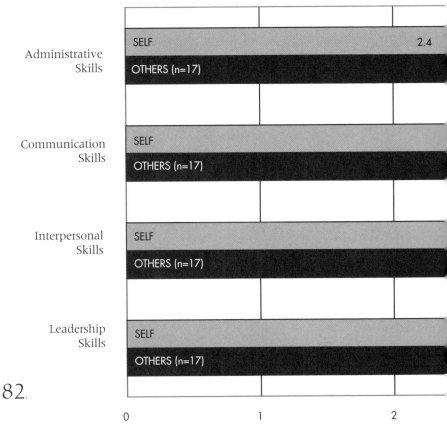

Administrative Skills	SELF	2.4
	OTHERS (n=17)	
Communication Skills	SELF	
	OTHERS (n=17)	
Interpersonal Skills	SELF	
	OTHERS (n=17)	
Leadership Skills	SELF	
	OTHERS (n=17)	

0   1   2

Not Applicable = 0,   Strongly Disagree = 1,   Disagree = 2,

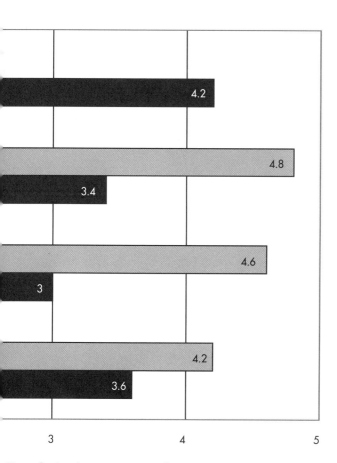

3   4   5

Neutral = 3,   Agree = 4,   Strongly Agree = 5

Stephen's Competency Averages by Each Rater Category

Administrative Skills
- SELF — 2.4
- BOSS (n=1)
- DIRECT REPORTS (n=10)
- PEERS (n=6)

Communication Skills
- SELF
- BOSS (n=1)
- DIRECT REPORTS (n=10)
- PEERS (n=6)

Interpersonal Skills
- SELF
- BOSS (n=1)
- DIRECT REPORTS (n=10)
- PEERS (n=6)

Leadership Skills
- SELF
- BOSS (n=1)
- DIRECT REPORTS (n=10)
- PEERS (n=6)

0   1   2

84.

Not Applicable = 0,   Strongly Disagree = 1,   Disagree = 2,

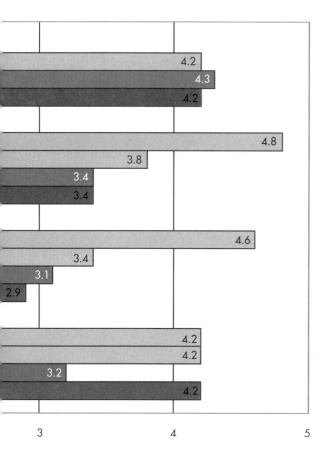

3   4   5

85.

Neutral = 3,   Agree = 4,   Strongly Agree = 5

Stephen's Item Level Ratings (Administrative Skills)

1. Establishes comprehensive plans

SELF	2
BOSS (n=1)	
DIRECT REPORTS (n=10)	
PEERS (n=6)	

2. Manages multiple priorities

SELF	
BOSS (n=1)	
DIRECT REPORTS (n=10)	
PEERS (n=6)	

3. Adjusts plans to respond to changing priorities

SELF	
BOSS (n=1)	
DIRECT REPORTS (n=10)	
PEERS (n=6)	

4. Uses information effectively

SELF	2
BOSS (n=1)	
DIRECT REPORTS (n=10)	
PEERS (n=6)	

5. Allocates resources efficiently

SELF	2
BOSS (n=1)	
DIRECT REPORTS (n=10)	
PEERS (n=6)	

0   1   2

86.

Not Applicable = 0, Strongly Disagree = 1, Disagree = 2,

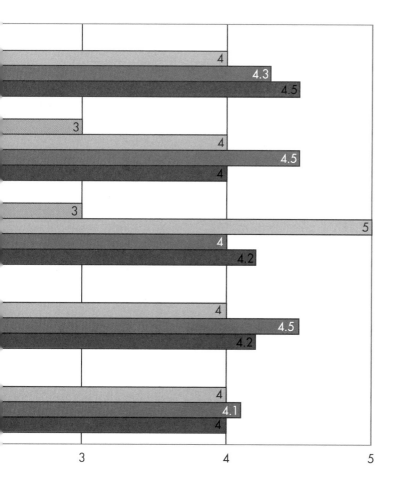

Neutral = 3,   Agree = 4,   Strongly Agree = 5

Table 1

Stephen's Remaining Item Level Ratings by Each Rater

Competency/Item

Communication Skills

6. Is easily understood

7. Listens without interrupting

8. Clearly expresses ideas in writing

9. Appropriately tailors message to audience

10. Delivers effective presentations

Interpersonal Skills

11. Respects all people, regardless of their background

12. Expresses disagreements tactfully

13. Is open to different viewpoints

14. Promotes positive relationships

15. Uses a positive approach when faced with conflict

Leadership Skills

16. Assigns projects that provide development opportunities

17. Provides clear direction

18. Delegates tasks to the appropriate people

19. Influences others by asserting his/her views

20. Is decisive when necessary

Not Applicable = 0, Strongly Disagree = 1, Disagree = 2,

Category

Self (n=1)	Boss (n=1)	Direct Reports (n=10)	Peers (n=6)
5	5	4	4.3
5	4	1.8	3.2
5	4	4.4	4
4	2	2.5	2.8
5	4	4.5	2.7
5	4	2.8	3.2
4	3	2.8	2.8
5	3	2.9	2.8
5	4	3.5	3.2
4	3	3.4	3.2
5	4	2	3.8
4	5	2.9	4
4	5	1.8	3.8
3	4	4.6	4.5
5	3	4.7	4.8

89.

Neutral = 3, Agree = 4, Strongly Agree = 5

ENDNOTES

1 360° feedback is a registered trademark of TEAMS, Inc.

2 BENCHMARKS® (Center for Creative Leadership), Campbell Leadership Index® (NCS Assessments), Competency Portfolio℠ (Hay/McBer), Leader Behavior Analysis II™ (Blanchard Training and Development), Leadership Competencies for Managers© (Clark L. Wilson, Ph.D., distributed by The Booth Co.), Leadership/Impact™ (Human Synergystics/Center for Applied Research, Inc.), The PROFILOR® (Personnel Decisions International), and VOICES® (Lominger Limited).

3 London, M. and J. Smither (1995).

4 Peters, T. (1999).

5 O'Reilly, B. (1994).

6 Lepsinger, R. and A. Lucia (1997).

7 Peterson, D. and M. Hicks (1995).

8 Brutus, S., J. Fleenor, and M. London (1998).

9 See Edwards, M. and A. Ewen (1996). And Johnson, J. and A. Olson (1996).

10 Brutus, S., J. Fleenor, and M. London (1998).

11 See London, M. (1997) for a discussion of common rater errors.

12 Paradise-Tornow, C. (1998).

13 DeBare, I. (1997).

14 London, M. (1997).

15 Charan, R. and G. Colvin (1999).

16 Kirkland, K. and S. Manoogian (1998).

17 See Hammond, S. (1996) for more on using an Appreciative Inquiry approach.

18 Davis, B., S. Gebelein, L. Hellervik, J. Sheard, and C. Skube (Eds.). (1996).

19 Kirkland, K. and S. Manoogian (1998).

20 See Lombardo, M. and R. Eichinger (1989) for more on how overused strengths can become weaknesses.

21 See Hezlett, S. and B. Koonce (1995).

22 Davis, B., S. Gebelein, L. Hellervik, J. Sheard, and C. Skube (Eds.). (1996).

23 Gebelein, S., K. Nelson-Neuhaus, E. Sloan, and D. Lee (1999).

24 Lombardo, M. and R. Eichinger (1998).

25 O'Reilly, B. (1994).

26 Bracken, D., M. Dalton, R. Jako, C. McCauley, and V. Pollman (1997). And Bracken, D., C. Timmreck, and A. Church (Eds.). (Forthcoming).

27 Dalton, M. (1998).

28 See Van Velsor, E., J. Leslie, and J. Fleenor (1997) for a more in-depth discussion of these issues.

29 Van Velsor, E., J. Leslie, and J. Fleenor (1997).

91.

REFERENCES

Bracken, D., C. Timmreck, and A. Church (Eds.). (Forthcoming). The Handbook of MultiSource Feedback. Jossey-Bass Publishers: San Francisco, California.

Bracken, D., M. Dalton, R. Jako, C. McCauley, and V. Pollman. (1997). Should 360-Degree Feedback Be Used Only for Developmental Purposes? Center for Creative Leadership: Greensboro, North Carolina.

Brutus, S., J. Fleenor, and M. London. (1998). "Elements of Effective 360-Degree Feedback." In Tornow, W., M. London, and CCL Associates (Eds.). Maximizing the Value of 360-Degree Feedback. Jossey-Bass Publishers: San Francisco, California.

Charan, R. and G. Colvin (1999). "Why CEOs Fail." Fortune, June 21, pages 69-78.

Dalton, M. (1998). "Best Practices: Five Rationales for Using 360-Degree Feedback in Organizations." In Tornow, W., M. London, and CCL Associates (Eds). Maximizing the Value of 360-Degree Feedback. Jossey-Bass Publishers: San Francisco, California.

Davis, B., S. Gebelein, L. Hellervik, J. Sheard, and C. Skube (Eds.). (1996). Successful Manager's Handbook: Development Suggestions for Today's Managers. Personnel Decisions International: Minneapolis, Minnesota.

DeBare, I. (1997). "360-Degrees of Evaluation: More Companies Turning to Full-Circle Job Reviews." San Francisco Chronicle, Monday, May 5.

Edwards, M. and A. Ewen. (1996). 360° Feedback. AMACOM: New York.

Gebelein, S., K. Nelson-Neuhaus, E. Sloan, and D. Lee. (1999). Successful Executive's Handbook. Personnel Decisions International: Minneapolis, Minnesota.

Hammond, S. (1996). The Thin Book of Appreciative Inquiry. Thin Book Publishing Co.: Plano, Texas.

Johnson, J. and A. Olson. (1996). "Implementing Multiple Perspective Feedback: An Integrated Framework." Human Resources Management Review, Vol. 6, Issue 4, pages 253-278.

Hezlett, S. and B. Koonce. (1995). "Now that I've Been Assessed, What Do I Do? Facilitating Development after Individual Assessments." Paper presented at the IPMA Assessment Council Conference on Public Personnel Assessment, New Orleans, LA.

Kirkland, K. and S. Manoogian. (1998). Ongoing Feedback: How to Get It, How to Use It. Center for Creative Leadership: Greensboro, North Carolina.

Lepsinger, R. and A. Lucia. (1997). The Art & Science of 360° Feedback. Jossey-Bass Pfeiffer: San Francisco, California.

Lombardo, M. and R. Eichinger. (1989). Preventing Derailment: What to Do Before It's Too Late. Center for Creative Leadership: Greensboro, North Carolina.

Lombardo, M. and R. Eichinger. (1998). For Your Improvement: A Development and Coaching Guide. Lominger Limited, Inc.: Minneapolis, Minnesota.

London, M. (1997). Job Feedback: Giving, Seeking, and Using Feedback for Performance Improvement. Lawrence Erlbaum Associates: Mahwah, New Jersey.

London, M. and J. Smither. (1995). "Can Multi-Source Feedback Change Perceptions of Goal Accomplishment, Self-Evaluations, and Performance-Related Outcomes?" Personnel Psychology, Vol. 48, Issue 4, pages 803-840.

O'Reilly, B. (1994). "360 Feedback Can Change Your Life." Fortune, October, 17, pages 93-97.

Paradise-Tornow, C. (1998). "The Competitive Advantage of Customer Involvement in 360-Degree Feedback." In Tornow, W., M. London, and CCL Associates (Eds.). Maximizing the Value of 360-Degree Feedback. Jossey-Bass Publishers: San Francisco, California.

Peters, T. (1999). Reinventing Work: The Brand You 50. Alfred A. Knopf, Inc.: New York.

Peterson, D. and M. Hicks. (1995). Development First: Strategies for Self-Development. Personnel Decisions International: Minneapolis, Minnesota.

Van Velsor, E., J. Leslie, and J. Fleenor. (1997). Choosing 360: A Guide to Evaluating Multi-Rater Feedback Instruments for Management Development. Center for Creative Leadership: Greensboro, North Carolina.

ACKNOWLEDGMENTS

I would like to thank the many people who took time to read drafts of this *Thin Book on 360 Feedback*. Their input, expertise, and unique perspectives are reflected in these pages: Eugenia E. Acosta, J.D., John Adcock, Lia Bosch, David W. Bracken, Ph.D., David G. Brenner, Belinda Butler, James Cornick, Cornelius T. "Neil" Fletcher, Bruce Halliday, Laura Hammill, Ph.D., Rand Hammond, Hank Jonas, Ph.D., Paul E. Larson, Larry L. Looker, Vonda K. Mills, Ph.D., Leah Chevalier Mouton , Linda K. Mowder, Nancy E. Polk, Ph.D., James R. Powers, Ph.D., Keith Rettig, Marlene Roundtree, Cathy Royal, Ph.D., Nancy Schreiber, Ph.D., Linne Shields, Thomas E. Shields, Ph.D., John Singer, Ph.D., Al Stroud, Scott Taylor, Carol Timmreck, Kenneth M. Tinsley, Carole Townsley, and Deedra Yarbrough. There were also reviewers who wished to remain anonymous. I would also like to thank Shannon Evans, Laurie Fry, Rand Hammond and Leah Chevalier Mouton for seeking input from managers at their companies. I owe a special thanks to Sue Annis Hammond and Keith Rettig. Sue, the publisher of the Thin Book Series, provided the opportunity and guidance that made this book a reality. Keith, of multirater.com, helped me understand the future of 360 Feedback technology.

Finally, I would like to thank my husband, Stephen Rodrigues, and my son, Stephen, for their unwavering patience and support.

— MLC

About the Author

Michelle LeDuff Collins is a consultant who specializes in management assessments and management development. She brings more than ten years of experience to the human resources field from her work with The City of New Orleans, Personnel Decisions International, American Airlines, and The Associates. She received her Ph.D. in industrial/organizational psychology from Tulane University in 1994, and has been providing consulting services to organizations since 1998.

For more information about her consulting services, visit www.hrdevelopment.org or e-mail her at michellecollins@thinbook.com.

Thin Book Publishing Co. Order Form

ORDERLINE: 888.316.9544

FAX: 972.403.0065

PHONE: 972.378.0523

TO ORDER ONLINE
www.thinbook.com

TO ORDER BY MAIL:
Thin Book Publishing Co.
PO Box 260608
Plano, TX 75026-0608

The Thin Book 360 Feedback: A Manager's Guide
— *Michelle LeDuff Collins*

$10.95 for one

$9.95 for 10-50

$9.00 for 51+

The Thin Book of Appreciative Inquiry
— *Sue Annis Hammond*

$7.95 for one

$6.95 for 10-50

$6.50 for 51+

Check _____

Credit Card Account No. _____
(American Express, VISA, Mastercard)

Signature (required)

_____   Expiration Date _____

U.S. Shipping: $2.50 each book, $.50 per each additional. Shipping is discounted for quantity orders. Express shipping also available. 8.25% sales tax for sales within Texas.

Name: _____

Company Name: _____

Address: _____

_____

_____

Phone: _____   Fax Phone: _____